# hOw₂ wAsTe tImE bRilLiAntLY

**a book by dELiA*s & C. Weigl**

Thanks to all the creative
critters who shared their ideas
with me for this book:

William Alba
Celia Bland
D. Victor Maxwell
Carol Mirakove
Andrew Nahem
Polly Shulman
Christopher Sey

And much appreciation to
the dELiA*s crew who
did the groovy illustrations:

Leslie Goldman
Abby Jacobs
Jason Willhoit Roe

email us at **how2@delias.com**

**Published by dELiA*s**
435 Hudson St., New York, NY 10014
©2001 by dELiA*s/ C. Weigl
Manufactured in the United States of America.
All rights reserved.
ISBN 0-9706304-2-5
Library of Congress Control Number: 00-136737

# YoUr WaKe-uP CaLL

Are you bored? Does the world sometimes seem designed to put you to sleep? That just means it's time to start making your own alarm clocks...really loud ones.

This book contains over 140 projects designed to stimulate your brain cells and inspire you to new heights of creative genius—plus tales of people who've made careers of combating monotony. **Declare war on the doldrums!** Make your life into a continual work of art! The ideas ahead range from sort-of-practical to totally ridiculous, but they all have one goal in mind: energizing your life by improving reality and making the world a more interesting place for everyone.

But first, a word to the wisegal: be nice. There's nothing brilliant about being mean or having fun at someone else's expense. Real cleverness means opening minds, doing cool things for people, broadening possibilities, and generally making life more exciting (or at least funnier).

So, read on and **turn boredom into brilliance!**

**oF sOuNd mInD?** Give your day an outlandish soundtrack. Make tapes of ambient noises and listen to them as you go about your daily routine. Plan ahead for maximum mind-bending effects. Make a tape of subway sounds to listen to during a long car trip. Do your homework to the sound of a cheering crowd. Listen to a ping pong game while you take a bath.

PaY tHe toLl oR bUs FaRe fOr tHe PeRsoN bEhInD YoU.

**wOrDs oF wIsDoM.** In your battle against boredom, beware of clichés. They are booby traps designed to fry our brains with worn-out, meaningless proverbs. The next time someone assaults your sanity with a cliché, fight fire with fire by inventing one that's even more ridiculous. If someone tells you "The early bird gets the worm," respond with "Yes, but the ink never dries if your pen is filled with lard." Try to say it with a straight face.

**nAmE aLL tHe tReEs oN YoUr bLoCk.**

**sUrPrIsE!** Open a box of cereal and replace the prize it offers with one of your own. Carefully reseal everything and leave it for your little brother or roommate to find at breakfast tomorrow. Nothing gross or toxic, okay? Stick to safe stuff like a CD, funny photos, or a personal message.

h0w2

dELiA*s

**sWeEt nOtHinGs** Call friends' and relatives' answering machines, disguise your voice, and say "I love you" as sincerely as possible.

wRiTe a LeTteR tO YoUr fUtuRe seLf. dOn'T rEaD iT aGaIn fOr 5 YeArS.

**eYeS biGGeR tHaN sToMaChS.**
Have fun with food coloring. Make a delicious meal for your family, but dye it with bright and unsettling colors. Pink mashed potatoes! Green macaroni and cheese! Finish off with a black dessert.

**sPrEaD tHe wOrD.** Enlist your friends to help you spread new slang words. See how long they take to catch on. Experiment with different sorts of words (insulting, complimentary, words that describe emotions, complete nonsense). See if certain types of words spread faster than others.

*That sale was a total **buffet.***

*My mom keeps trying to get all **puritan** on my clothes.*

*She was blazing at **factor 4.***

**bAcKwArDs LYrIcS** Choose a song and "translate" the lyrics, word by word, into their opposite. For instance, "You are my sunshine" would become "I ain't your darkness." Make sure the new words fit the old rhythm and start singing.

cArVe a bLocK oF cHeEsE tO LoOk LiKe a bAr oF sOaP.

h0w2

dELiA'S

**bY tHe bOoK.** Create a library...of books by you! Head to a thrift store or yard sale and buy a cheap hardcover book. Take it home and start transforming it. Cover it with your own artwork. Paste photos and other images over some of the pages. Paint or draw on others. Glue in your own poems and stories or black out various words on the existing page to create your own masterpiece.

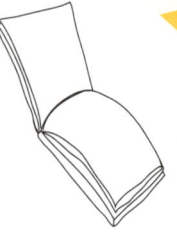

**LeAvE a fLoWeR oN eVeRY mAiLbOx YoU sEe tOdAY.**

**NaNcY DrEw fOr a DaY.** Follow one of your friends around all day. Make sure you're not spotted. Go home and write a detailed surveillance report of her activities. The next day, casually mention one or two of the things she did. If she asks how you know, hand her a copy of the report.

**dIG iT!** Fill strangers with hope! Draw a map that will lead them to a buried treasure. Leave your map in a place where it will take a little while before anyone finds it, like under a lamp in a hotel room (which is one way to pass time during those family vacations) or hidden in a book at the library. Don't dash their hopes: really leave something for them to find at the end of your trail.

**iNvEnT YoUr oWn LanGuAGe.**

hOw2
dELiA's *

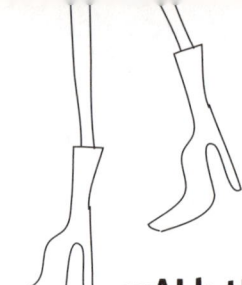

**wALk tHiS wAY.** Go to the mall and find someone with an interesting walk. Stroll along behind her and imitate the way she moves. The point isn't to mock anyone. Acting teachers use this exercise to help their students get into their roles. So, treat it as an acting exercise; be subtle and don't get caught. Continue until you find someone new to tail.

sTaRt sInG-aLonGs aT iNaPProPrIaTe mOmEnts.

**tHe nAmE oF tHe GaMe.** Feeling playful? Invent your own games! You can make things more interesting by coming up with the name first and then making up the rules. Some names you can start with: Green Fuzz, Lame Excuses, Power Flirting.

**GrOw uP.** Try this one out on your mother. Buy three potted plants. They should be the same kind of plant in the same kind of pot, but the plants themselves should be different sizes (small, medium and large). Give mom the smallest plant as a gift. A day or two later, secretly replace it with the medium-sized plant. Wait again and then do the same thing with the biggest plant. Mom will think she has the green thumb of a superhero…until you reverse the process and make the plant shrink again!

**cOvEr YoUr bEdRoOm wAlLs wItH sHaG cArPeTinG.**

**sEnSeLeSs.** Spend a few hours without one of your senses or limbs. Blindfold yourself. Wear earplugs. Put on a pair of thick gloves so you can't feel anything. Tie one hand behind your back. Hop around on one foot.

LeAvE fUnNY fOrTuNeS foLdEd uP iN tHe cOiN rEtUrN sLoTs oF PaYPhoNeS.

 **sHoTs iN tHe dArK.** Gather a group of friends in a completely dark room. Give each one of them a disposable camera and let them start shooting. Let chaos rule or take turns. You'll get a momentary glimpse (flash!) and a permanent record of what your pals do when the lights go out, not to mention some great art!

12
✹ 13

**reAd tHe LaBeL.** Embarrassment builds character...at least, that's what you should tell whoever you play this trick on. Use your computer to create fake address labels with your friend's name and address—the kind that magazines use to mail issues to their subscribers. Use a real one as a guide and make yours as convincing as possible by including things like phony customer ID numbers and mailing codes. Stick the label on magazines that your pal is least likely to read (or would be most embarrassed to have people think she reads). If she's the hardcore athletic type, turn her into a *Ladies Home Journal* subscriber. If she's quiet and shy, slap her name on *Corvette Fever*. Leave the evidence around for others to find.

caLl YoUr PaReNtS aNd teLl tHeM YoU'vE JoInEd tHe cIrCuS.

h0w 2

dELiA*s *

**bLoW oUt.** Does someone make you wait in the car a lot? Retaliate and entertain yourself at the same time! With the car engine off, fill the driver-side air conditioning/heating vents with confetti. Point the vents toward your intended victim and switch the fan to its highest setting. Sit back and watch what happens when she turns the key.

BuY sOmEtHiNg You cAn'T iMaGiNe wEaRing...aNd tHeN wEaR iT.

**siGn uP.** There's nothing more cruel or immature than sticking a "Kick Me" sign on someone's back. But that doesn't rule out the possibility of sticking something else on your own! Why not turn the idea around and put a nice suggestion on your back like, "Say Something Sweet" or "Blow Me a Kiss."

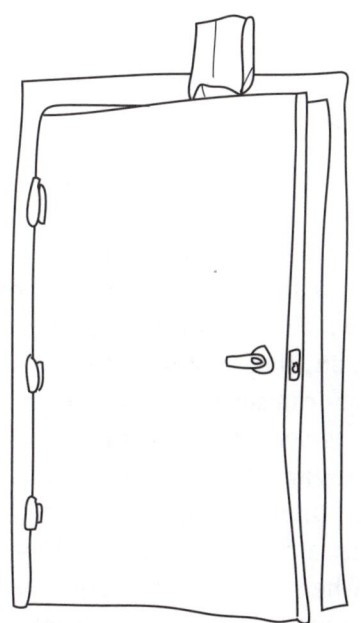

**mOrE cOnFetTi.** Instead of the old, bucket-of-water-over-the-door trick (which can hurt someone, ruin clothing and get you in BIG trouble), use a paper bag filled with popcorn, glitter or ping pong balls. Tape the bottom of the bag to the top of the door so it spills on whomever enters.

CaLl a fRiEnD aNd teLl hEr sHe'S wOn a LiFeTimE-suPPLY oF saLaMaNdErS.

**make a career of it!**

**tHe sUrReALiStS** were a zany bunch of artists and writers who liked inventing mind-warping games to pass the time. One of their best language games is called "The Exquisite Corpse." Players have a sheet of paper in front of them, at the top of which they write a definite or indefinite article (a, an, the). Everyone folds their paper, so no one can see what they wrote, and passes it to the person sitting next to them. Now each player writes an adjective, folds and passes again. This continues as the players add a noun, a verb, another article, another adjective and another noun. When finished, everyone unfolds their pages and reads the strange sentences they've created. The first sentence **the Surrealists** came up with this way was "The exquisite corpse shall drink the new wine" ...hence the game's name.

[Hey! If you like this sort of thing, check out another nifty dELiA*s book: *How2 Write Love Poems That Don't Suck.*]

wEaR YoUr bAtHiNG sUiT uNdEr eVeRYtHiNG, "JuSt iN cAsE."

**dReSs YoUr doG uP aNd tAkE hIm tO tHe PrOm aS YoUr dAtE.**

# tHe bRiDe oF eXQuIsItE cOrPsE.

You can also do a visual version of the Exquisite Corpse game by drawing pictures instead of writing words. This time, when you fold the paper and pass it on, leave a little bit of your drawing showing for the next player to see. It shouldn't be enough for him to figure out what you drew—just about 1/4 of an inch or so. Now he must draw something, starting with whatever lines you've let carry over into his section. Continue until the page is filled and unfold it to reveal your collective work of art.

**tAkE nOtE.** Have personalized stationery or notepads made with your friend's name on them. Write bizarre notes or shopping lists and leave them in public places. Or make some kooky stationery for yourself. Write official letters from imaginary companies like "Home for Friendless Thoughts" or "Snooze Alarm, Inc."

hAnD oUt fLYeRs fOr fAkE eVeNtS.

*From the desk of Lisa Williams*
- Pick up Denture Cream
- Call Russian Embassy
- DON'T FORGET TUBA LESSON!

Home for Friendless Thoughts

**fReEdOm oF cHoIcE.** Pass the time and explore the hidden corners of people's minds by playing "Would You Rather?" Players take turns asking one another either/or questions. If you do it well, you can learn your friends' hopes and dreams ("would you rather find true love or $1,000,000?"), what's important to them ("would you rather give up your computer or your phone?"), and what embarrasses them ("would you rather get caught singing in the mirror or spying on your crush?"). Toss out some weird questions to spice things up ("would you rather shrink or grow one inch per year for the rest of your life?"). Some more examples to get you started:

*Would you rather*
   always lose or never play?
   **be normal and ignored or brilliant and disliked?**
   give up sleeping or eating?
   **have glass walls in your bathroom or bedroom?**
   have one wish granted today or three wishes granted ten years from now?
   **know it all or have it all?**
   wear shoes full of worms or a hat full of spiders?

LeArN oLd dAnCeS LiKe tHe hUsTLe oR tHe PonY. tEaCh tHem tO YoUr PareNtS.

**A fAmiLiaR rInG.** Trapped at home with your sister? Need something to pass the time? How about a clock? Get two battery-powered digital alarm clocks. Set each to go off in five minutes and hide them somewhere in one another's rooms. Return to your own room and start searching. Whoever can't find their clock before it rings has to do the other's chores for a week...or clean her room...or call her "Oh Great and Exalted Sister" for the rest of her life.

**bOuNcY cHeCkS.** Do you write checks? Never leave the "memo" section blank. It's the perfect place to write cryptic messages, fortunes, trivia questions or anything else you want. Send cheerful notes to utility companies like "Love your gas!" or "You brighten my day!"

dEVeLoP a rEaLlY aNnoYinG hAbIt.

**bLaSt fRoM tHe PaSt.** Make a list of the people you remember from your first grade class. Decide who you liked best, who was the cutest, who you were afraid of, who was the funniest. Track each person down and tell them. If you don't feel like being that honest, just use the internet to track down people you haven't seen since you were a little kid. Write to them and find out how much (or little) they've changed.

**TaLk tO YoUrSeLf.** Do a search on the internet and find as many people as you can who share your name. Email them all. Ask for their life stories. Do you all have anything in common besides your name?

FiLl tHe bAtHtUb wItH saLt wAtEr aNd PrEtEnD iT's tHe oCeAn.

**BiG wOrDs.** Enervated? Suffering from ennui and lassitude? Spend an afternoon looking up all those annoying SAT test vocabulary words whose meanings you've never been sure about. Start using them in your regular conversations. Anyone who understands what you're saying will admire your perspicacity.

**CaLl mE NaMeS.** Choose a new name for yourself and insist that everyone use it. When you've succeeded, choose a new one and repeat the process. See how many names you can cycle through before people get fed up.

rEPLaCe aLl tHe nOuNs iN a sTorY wItH tHe nAmEs oF coLoRs aNd rEaD iT aLoUd.

h0w2

dELiA*s *

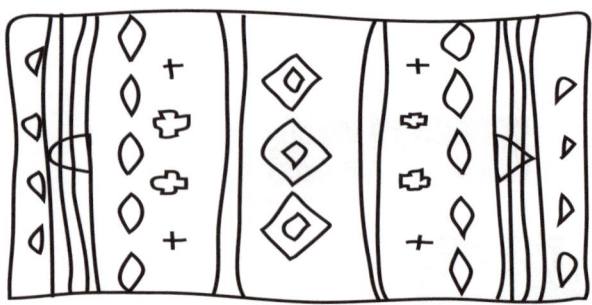

**LiE LiKe a RuG.** Start a completely false rumor **about yourself.** See how fast it spreads and if the details mutate as it gets passed along. After you reveal that it was a hoax, talk to people and try to trace the path your fabrication traveled as it spread. Who told whom? Draw a rumor map and see who's the biggest gossip.

aLwaYs bRinG 2 dAtEs...iN cAsE oNe tUrnS oUt tO bE bOrInG.

**GeT tHe PiCtUrE?** Cut a photograph into jigsaw-puzzle pieces. Anonymously mail one piece to each of your friends (or any group of people who know one another). See if they manage to figure out that they all got one and put the pieces together.

8

THE FOCUS

Aliens Abduct Cheerleading Squad

ANN ARBOR - Some of our happiest moments in dreamland can occur when we're flying. Soaring above the world can leave us feeling liberated and powerful, as if we've escaped everything that has been weighing us down. The person in the dream above used flying to rise above the danger that was pursuing her. As often happens in dreams like this, she first realized that she **could** fly and then she did it...with a little bit of effort. This could be her way of telling herself that, if he works at it, her problems will become small and insignificant. She just has to break free of whatever internal or external forces are holding her down...and ignore the common-sense rules that say she can't rise above it all.

Of course, the meaning of your flying dream could be entirely different. It depends on many things:

How do you feel as you soar above the earth? Elated and free and "on top of the world?" Nervous about crashing? Barely able to stay afloat, no matter how hard you try?

What kind of flyer are you? Do you zoom like a fighter jet? Float like a leaf? Are you in control of where you're going or just heading wherever the wind blows you?

Why are you flying? To escape something on the ground? To get a better perspective on things? To get to a particular destination? For the pure joy of it?

*'m standing on top of a tall office building downtown. There must have been an earthquake or something, because the building starts tilting as if one side of it is sinking into the ground. I start sliding toward the edge of the roof. There are people on the building across the street, but they don't seem to hear my screams. I hold onto the very edge of the building for a few moments, but then I lose my*

Unfortunately, what goes up must come down. For most people, dreams of falling are more common than dreams of flying...which sucks because they're usually a lot less pleasant. Falling dreams can make us feel helpless and out of control. If that's the case with your dream, you should ask yourself in what areas of your life do you feel out of control? Often, other elements of the dream will give you a clue. In the dream above, the dreamer might be worried about work, because she's standing on—and then falling

off—an office building. She also seems to feel as if the people around her (her coworkers?) are ignoring her pleas for help.

To understand your falling dream, it might help to ask what you're worried about falling from, or into, in your waking life. Do you feel like you're falling out of grace with your friends? Is your self-esteem taking a nose-dive? Are you falling into someone's trap? Falling for

Looking on the bright side, maybe you're taking a more desirable tumble—like falling in love. That can leave us feeling helpless and happy at the same time, so pay close attention to your feelings in the dream. In fact, some falling dreams feel kind of good. We might be terrified as we cling to the side of a cliff, but then feel relieved when we finally lose our grip and take the plunge. A dream like that might be about learning to "let go."*'m sitting by myself at a corner table in a crowded restaurant. I'm totally embarrassed*

*because I'm completely naked, but so far no one seems to notice. I'm trying to figure out how to get up and leave without anyone seeing me, when the waiter brings me a big plate of spaghetti. Now I'm really nervous, because I know that I have to eat it but if I drip any sauce on myself that will somehow cause people to see my nakedness.*

There probably isn't a person on this planet who hasn't dreamed

of being naked in public. And, as in this dream, the main emotions are often fear and embarrassment. We might feel vulnerable and exposed and try desperately to cover ourselves up, to hide ourselves from others. Occasionally, though, we just sit there calmly and wonder why nobody has picked up on the fact that we're letting it all hang out.

In general, when you're naked in a dream, you've dropped all masks and defenses and are exposing your true self for others to see. Obviously, this can be scary, but it can also mean many other things. Next time you have a dream like this, try asking yourself the following questions:

When do you feel exposed in your waking life?

Are you hoping to be noticed? By whom? Or would you rather just fade into the scenery? Why? Is there someone you wish you could open up to and express your real feelings? Does that worry you?

You should also pay attention the details of the dream, because they might tip you off to the part of your life the dream is addressing. Where are you? At school? On a picnic with your family? On a bus? How do people react to the naked truth you're showing them? Do they laugh? Are they grossed out? Do they totally ignore you?

In the case of the dream above, the dreamer is in a restaurant where she's going to have to eat a plate of spaghetti. She doesn't want to because it will call attention to her. Does this mean that she feels like the things she needs to nourish and sustain herself (mentally? spiritually?) are going to expose her to the criticism of others? Or does she feel as if she can't handle her responsibilities (what's "on her plate") and people

**"In the world above, the aliens might be worried about work, because she's standing on their shoulders she is good."**
**—B. Dohrn**

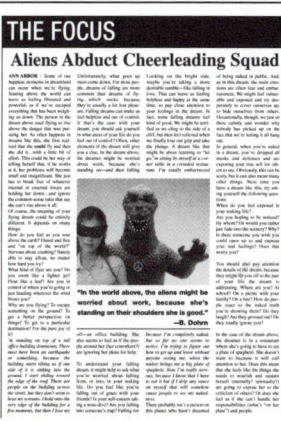

**MaKe tHe nEwS.** Use your computer to create a fake newspaper article that's sure to cause a stir...or a laugh. Make photocopies and hang them up around your school. Write an article about the School Board's decision to extend the school day by three hours or about how you won a national award for your contributions to the field of Theoretical Physics. As always, don't write anything dumb or mean. And don't spread lies about other people...unless you have their permission.

**sPeNd a daY LaUGhInG eVerY hOuR oN tHe hOuR.**

Obsession is a great way to waste time. Of course, if you're going to obsess, you might as well make it interesting. Some of the most fascinating—and creative—obsessions can be seen in works of American folk artists. Here are two possible role models for you: **tReSsA PrIsbReY** was 60 years old when she was bought a 1/3-acre lot in Simi Valley, California. Over the next 25 years, she built 13 buildings and over 20 large sculptures on her property—including shrines, walkways and wishing wells—out of hundreds of thousands of bottles! She chose to use bottles because they were a cheap building material...and they gave her someplace to store her collection of 17,000 pencils.

**oPeN eVerY dOoR, cAbInEt, cLoSeT aNd dRaWeR iN YoUr hOuSe**

make a career of it!

**hEnRY dArGeR** lived in the same small, one-room apartment in Chicago for 40 years. When he passed away in 1972, his landlord found collections of Pepto-Bismol® bottles and thousands of balls of string in his apartment. He also found a 19,000 page book Henry had written and hundreds of watercolor paintings that illustrated scenes from the book. Some of the paintings were huge murals on stitched-together bed sheets; many of them have been shown in museums across the country.

So go overboard! Start a huge collection of "useless" stuff. Keep a diary of your dreams or of the daily weather patterns. People might call you crazy, but you might also get into the record books... or an art gallery.

wAiT fOr sOmEoNe tO cOmE hOmE. PrEtEnD nOt tO nOtIcE.

hOw2

dELiA*s ✻

**sPeAk uP.** Leave messages, poems and manifestos everywhere. Fold them up and slip them into the coin return slots of payphones and vending machines. Remove napkins from dispensers in restaurants, write notes and fortunes on two or three, and then neatly replace them. Drop notes into people's bags at the mall. Hand them out on street corners.

BuY sOmEtHiNg tHaT's PeRfEcT fOr YoU...aNd GiVe iT aWaY.

**sTaR PoWeR.** Pretend you're famous. Always ride in the back of the car and don't get out until someone opens the door for you. Say "ciao" a lot. Wear big sunglasses, dress extravagantly and always ask for the best table...even at diners and fast food joints. Carry your dog everywhere. Have a hairdo. Call celebrities by their first names.

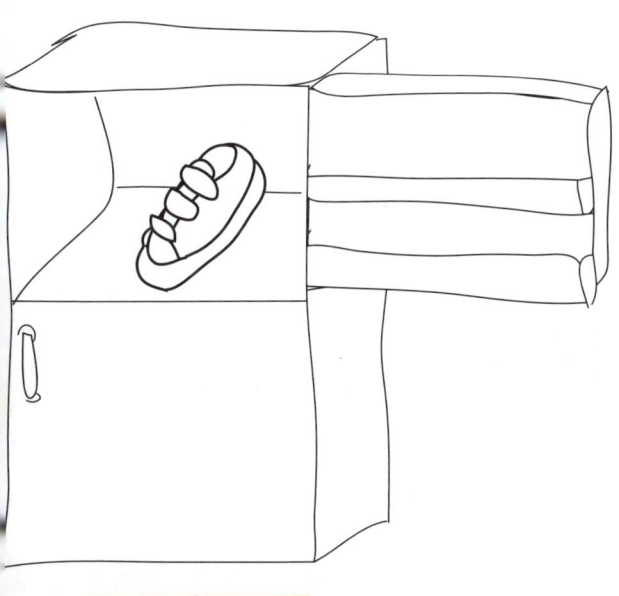

**LeArn tO PLaY tHe dRuMs...LoUdLY.**

# uNcOmMoN CoLd. Give someone a jolt of the unexpected by secretly putting a common object in the freezer. Take it out just before your experimental subject is likely to use it. Watch his face as his brain tries to process the fact that whatever it is (the newspaper, a pair of shoes, a toothbrush) is ice cold.

mAiL aN aNoNYmOuS LiKe PoEm tO sOmEoNe.

**dOuBLe TaKeS.** Get a couple of friends to agree that you will each wear a distinctive accessory to school or work, like a scarf, a bracelet or an unusual belt. The items should be something that people will notice, but not really focus on too closely. Throughout the day, without letting anyone see you, trade the items among yourselves. See if anyone notices that your accessories are moving from person to person. If someone does, deny everything. If you think you're good enough actors (or at least can lie with a straight face), try trading something more obvious, like your shirts.

**DiReCtoR's cHaIr.** Tired of lame, boring television shows? Use the "record" and "stop" buttons on your VCR to splice together your own personalized TV series, using fragments from a dozen different programs. Mix reality cop shows with Saturday morning cartoons or the news with one of those weird infomercials. Music videos work especially well.

**LeArN tO sPeAk eSPeRaNtO.**

**GrOw GrAfFiTi.** Write your name or a short message on your lawn with fertilizer. Water thoroughly. The grass where you put fertilizer will eventually be greener and healthier than the rest of the lawn.

hOw2

dELiA's *

**sELf-PuBLiSh.** Use your computer to create something that looks just like a page from a magazine your friend or someone in your family reads regularly. Match the font and the overall design style. You can write an article about yourself, create an absurd full-page ad, or come up with a story about a bizarre new fashion trend (complete with pictures). Glue your page over one of the pages in the magazine and wait for a reaction.

CaLl YoUrSeLf oN YoUr CeLl PhOnE fRoM a reGuLaR PhOnE. wHiSPeR sEcReTs.

**bRiGht iDeAs.** Become a one-girl complaint department. Put suggestion boxes on street corners, in your school, at bus stops, on your front porch. They should look as "official" as possible. Empty them out every week and see what people have to say. Make a complaint book. If you like someone's suggestion, try to implement it.

cHoOsE sOmE aTtrIbUtE oF a PaRtIcULaR aNiMaL aNd aDoPt iT fOr a wEeK.

**TaKe a tInT!** Wear clothes that are all one color. Only eat food of the same hue. Mention the color in as many conversations as possible. Become your color. Be green with envy. Start seeing red. Talk a blue streak.

### A rOsE bY AnY oThEr nAmE.
Plant flowers. Name each one. Have weekly birthday parties for them. Invite your friends.

cHoOsE a wOrD aNd tRY tO uSe iT aS mUcH aS PoSsIbLe tOdaY.

### PiCtUrE tHiS.
Hang with movie stars. Help your friends visit far-away lands. Make the President walk your dog. How? With a pair of scissors! Use them to cut people into—or out of—photos. Create "authentic" pictures of faux events. Of course, you could also go the high-tech route and use a scanner and Adobe PhotoShop™.

**hIt tHe rOaD.** Plan a road trip where you visit towns with weird names. Head to Stinking Bay, AK, or Knockemstiff, OH. Take a sad drive across Alabama from Hopeful to Loveless. Or plan a massive voyage that will take you from Noseville, NY, through Elbow, IL, and Kneeland, WI, all the way to Heady, MO. Be sure to steer clear of Accident, MD, and Panic, PA. Write an itinerary of your trip and send it to friends and family.

MaKe uP reAsOnS tO tHrOw PaRtIeS LiKe, "A bAbY sHoWeR fOr mY hAmStEr!"

dOn'T uSe a mIrRoR tOdAY. LoOk iN oThEr PeoPLe's fAcEs aNd iMaGiNe wHaT tHeY sEe.

## rEtUrN tO sEnDeR.

Hand out a stack of self-addressed stamped postcards. On one side, print a simple instruction like "Draw a self-portrait" or "Describe your favorite person." Send some to famous people or politicians (soften them up by telling them it's for a school project). Keep a scrapbook of what people mail back to you.

**bLaCk aNd wHiTe.** Always carry a black felt-tip pen and a bottle of correction fluid. Whenever you're stuck in a waiting room, pass the time by "revising" one of the newspapers or magazines that are lying around. Use your pen to black out words in articles until the remaining words form your very own poem. Use the correction fluid to white-out the dialog in comics and replace it with something funnier (to you at least).

tAkE uP aN uNuSuAL hObBY LiKe tAxIdErMY oR LiOn tAmInG.

**sEiZe tHe DaY.** Start a new national holiday. Make greeting cards for it and send them out every year. Write it on people's calendars. See how many people you can get to celebrate it...and then try to get the day off from school.

**sEeInG sTaRs.** Make up new signs for the Zodiac. Base your new astrological science on the personalities of you and your friends. Instead of names like Scorpio, Taurus and Libra, use the names of people you know—your favorite cartoon characters, movie stars or common household items. Start writing a weekly astrology column.

sEnD a mEsSaGe iN a bOtTLe vIa a hElIuM bAlLoOn.

**uNsEaSoNabLY wArM.** Tape the TV news in August. Play it back in the winter during a snowstorm. Act very excited and call your family into the room when the weather report comes on. Convince them that the weird weather must have something to do with global warming.

**dRaMa QuEeNs.** Invite two friends over. Before they get there, write a script of the conversation the three of you will have. Make three copies and hand them out when they arrive. One way to write your little drama is to have it start out as a normal conversation that gradually gets more and more ridiculous. Don't forget to include actions ("Natasha grabs a pillow and wears it on her head defiantly"). Invent over-the-top soap-opera narratives. Turn your friends (and yourself) into totally new characters.

wEaR tWo dIfFeReNt sHoEs.

sEe hOw mAnY mOvIeS YoU cAn sQuEeZe iNtO oNe wEeKeNd. eAt onLY PoPcoRn.

make a career of it!

For performance artist **bOnNiE sHeRk,** incongruity rules. She's made a career of creating strange environments and performances in some unlikely places.

She once did a performance called "Public Lunch" in which she sat in the Lion House at the San Francisco Zoo and at feeding time, ate a fancy catered meal.

She created a series of "Portable Parks"—complete with grass, animals and palm trees—that she would set up temporarily in urban spaces...like alongside highway off-ramps.

For one performance, she dressed up in formal attire and sat in a living room chair...in the middle of a garbage dump.

**sPoOkY suPPeR.** Send anonymous invitations to all your friends to meet at some creepy outdoor spot just before sundown (the woods; the cemetery gates; on the lawn of that old, abandoned house). Watch everyone nervously decide whether or not they should show up. Reward the brave ones by having the fixings for a late-night picnic hidden somewhere near the meeting place. Break the goodies out after everyone sweats through a few minutes of darkness.

cOuNt aLl YoUr tEeTh wItH YoUr tOnGuE.

hOw2

dELiA's

**sHuTtErBuGGY.** Get a camera and for one week, document random daily events. Label each photo ("Breakfast, Monday"; "Thursday, 3:07pm"; "Making the Bed") and put them in a scrapbook. Another way to do it is to simply take a photograph every 60 minutes, no matter what you're doing at the time. Keep a written record of where and when you snap the shutter. Take a picture every time you hear a car horn and collect them in an album titled "pictures of a car horn." Or you can take one picture at the same time every day.

aCt sO nIcE tHaT YoU mAkE eVeRYoNe sIcK.

**PoWeR cOrRuPtS?** Invent your own political party and run for mayor. Come up with a list of campaign promises. Send out press releases with fake endorsements from fake organizations. Hang posters. Make speeches. Get on the news...

In the middle of the campaign, expose yourself in an extravagant (and equally fake) scandal.

VOTE FOR HEATHER MATHEWS!
If elected, I promise to:
- Give tax cuts to any male who legally changes his name to Princess Isabella Curling Iron.
- Make all police officers dress like ballerinas.
- Let kids vote to rename the block they live on.

**JaCkPoT.** Create your own weekly lottery, but come up with something more interesting than cash prizes (which are probably illegal anyway, unless you live in Las Vegas). The winner could get to choose new names for all the losers. You could all chip in and throw a party in the winner's honor or allow her to choose one item from each of your wardrobes.

cArPeT YoUr rOoM wItH aStRoTuRf™.

**PiEcEs oF YoU.** Write your autobiography on a series of postcards. Stop each in mid-sentence and continue it on the next card. Mail them to friends, distant relatives, or complete strangers.

Go bAcKPaCkInG ThRoUGh YOuR hOuSe. rOaSt MaRsHmAlLoWs oN tHe sToVe.

**SiNcEreLY YoUrS.** Write warm, personal thank-you notes all the time. Give them to fast food workers, bus drivers, the papergirl, your dentist, the guy who reads your electric meter.

*dear busdriver*

*thanx*

**sEe sPoT rUn.** Make a fake lost-pet poster with a picture of an implausible animal on it. Your "pet" can be a real animal like an orangutan or a cow...or you can create a totally fantastic creature with the head of a dog, the body of a snake and wings. Give the lost critter a common name like "Fluffy" or "Spot" and offer a reward for its return. Don't put your phone number on the poster, unless you're prepared to hear from a lot of weirdoes—or to find an orangutan on your doorstep.

cHaNGe tHe tImE oN eVerY cLoCk YoU sEe.

hOw2

dELiA's

**aCtInG uP.** Get together with some friends and produce an instant play. Have everyone write ten or twenty lines of unrelated dialog on scraps of paper. Put the scraps in a hat and shake well. Redistribute them and read them to one another as if you are actors in a very disjointed play. (Mary: "Why are you acting like a three-year old?" Dana: "Mayonnaise is disgusting." Laurie: "Well, maybe you should try doing yoga."). Get into your roles. Make it as melodramatic as possible.

kEeP aN aUdIo-dIarY bY rEcOrDinG YoUr tHouGhTs oN taPe.

**cHaIn rEaCtIoN.** Words are great tools...and toys. Get out a pen and link as many of them together as you can, making sure that each word relates to the ones before and after it. Create phrases like: "Another world peace pipe dream come true to life" or "Mr. soldier of fortune cookie monster mash potato head." See how far you can go.

**cErAmIc JunGLe.** Move all the house plants into the bathroom. Fill the room with shower steam. Pretend you're in the jungle. Dress appropriately.

GiVe YoUr fAvOriTe PoSseSsiOn tO a fRiEnD.

**hOw tOuChInG.** Need a game for a slumber party? Collect a bunch of small objects—things like a contact lens case, a meat thermometer and a snow globe. Pass them around under a blanket and see if your friends can figure out what they are by touch alone.

**make a career of it!**

Avant-garde American composer **JoHn CaGe**, shook up the classical music world with some radical ideas about how to make music.

He wrote songs for "prepared piano" in which he'd attach small objects made of wood, metal and rubber to the piano's strings.

He composed a piece called "Imaginary Landscape No. 4" in which the instruments were 12 radios tuned at random.

He would use "chance operations" like rolling dice to decide what notes to play.

One of his most famous compositions was 4' 33". It consisted of four minutes and thirty-three seconds of silence.

In San Francisco, he did a performance in which he showed up an hour early for the show, played the whole concert by himself and then left before the audience arrived.

PrEteNd YoU'vE foRGoTtEn tHe dIfFeReNcE bEtWeEn nOuNs aNd vErBs.

**aRt MeLt.** Make a sculpture that will decay over time. Build it out of ice, ripe fruit, or something that will dissolve in the rain. Assemble it on a beach before the tide comes in. Take photos to document its slow demise.

LeArN mOrSe cOdE aNd uSe YoUr fOrK tO sEnD sEcReT mEsSaGeS dUrInG dInNeR.

hOw2

dELiA*s

**A WaY wItH wOrDs.** Stuck alone somewhere? Get out some paper and a pencil and pass the time with word games.

Start out with some anagrams—words and phrases in which you rearrange the letters to spell something else (like ELVIS...LIVES). See what anagrams you can make from your name (Drew Barrymore could change hers into Merry Wardrobe). Or write an anagramed letter to a friend in which you turn things like "Dear Linda. How's it going?" into "Darn ideal. Sing with goo?"

Now try some palindromes—words and phrases that are spelled the same backwards and forwards. Once you get past words like "mom" and "dad," palindromes are pretty tough, so you can waste lots of time. A few examples to get you primed:

**Lonely Tylenol**
**Evil Olive**
**Draw pupil's lip upward.**
**Do geese see God?**
**Go hang a salami, I'm a lasagna hog.** (which is the title of a book of palindromes by Jon Agee.)

sTaRt cOlLeCtiNG sOmEtHiNG rEaLlY GroSs Like uSeD cHeWinG GuM.

**hOLd, PLeAsE.** Have nice, long conversations with telemarketers. Be extra friendly and keep them on the phone for as long as possible. Make them laugh. At some point, pretend to put them on hold and keep repeating, "All of our customers are with other telemarketers right now. Your call is important to us, so please stay on the line." Before you hang up, ask for their home phone number so you can chat later.

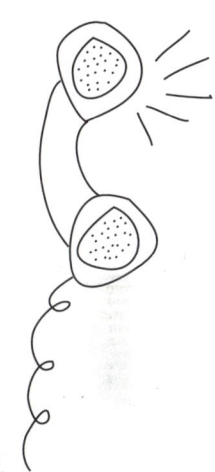

sTudY tHe sEcOnD LaW oF tHeRmOdYnAmIcs...tHeN fiGuRe oUt hOw tO dEfY iT.

make a career of it!

Author **vIrgiNiA wOoLf** once pulled a great prank on the British government by pretending that she was a visiting Indian dignitary. She dressed for the part and sent a telegram to London announcing her arrival. When she showed up, they gave her a formal reception and a tour of a British Navy vessel.

**GeT CaRdEd.** Print up little cards with silly sayings to hand out to people on the street. Some possibilities: "Play Nice," "Life is grand. Pass it on," and "You don't know me." Make a special batch for people who try to hand you flyers: "I'm sorry. I cannot accept flyers or leaflets at this time. Have a nice day."

rEcOrD tHe sOuNd oF sOmEthInG tHaT mAkEs YoU HaPPY. PLaY iT bAcK wHeN YoU'rE sAd.

Love is the message

# wHaT wAs tHe Question?

Next time you and your friends are hanging around with nothing to do, have each of them write a list of five questions and five answers on a sheet of paper. The questions and answers don't have to have anything to do with one another. Now take turns asking one another questions from your lists. Whoever you ask must answer with one of the answers they've already written down. The results can get pretty zany...and sometimes strangely revealing...

**Q: Why are you so mean?**
**A: Because there are no trees in the desert.**

**Q: What is love?**
**A: An internal organ that filters impurities from your bloodstream.**

You can also convert this game into a fortune-telling machine. Have everyone write several possible answers to a yes/no question on index cards (absolutely, no way, as certain as tomorrow's sunrise, not even if you were the last girl on earth, etc). Collect the cards, shuffle them and take turns asking yes/no questions about your future. Pick a card for your answer.

**i'M wItH tHe bAnD.** Start a band with a goofy name like Communist Love Child, Your Mom Ate My Homework, Ritual Tension, or Exposure of Reality Auto Club.

> wRiTe a PreTtY sOnG aBoUt sOmEtHinG dIsGuStInG.

**sEaRcH PaRtY.** Organize a scavenger hunt—not the lame kind you played at birthday parties in the second grade. Upgrade the idea for maximum hilarity and adventure. Establish teams and set a time limit (two to three hours works well). Now, come up with the list of items each team has to hunt down. They should be difficult, but not impossible to get, and they should require some ingenuity on the players' parts. Here's a sample list:

$1.37 worth of American cheese (this is especially good at night when there's only one

make a career of it!

The playwright, **aLfrEd JaRrY,** used to sit in the audience of his plays and "boo" loudly until he was thrown out of the theater.

wRiTe a fAsT sOnG aBoUt naPPinG. wRiTe an sIlLY sOnG aBouT bUtTeRfLiEs.

store still open that will slice an exact amount of cheese for you).

A bowling scorecard with at least one score below 100.

Something with the word "peace" on it.

A borrowed candy dish.

A discarded movie ticket to a particular film.

When the time is up, everybody returns to headquarters to compare their loot and their stories. The winner is the team that collects the most stuff. In the case of a tie, you'll have to vote on who did the most creative scavenging.

rEcOrD a cRiCkEt cHirPinG. PLaY tHE tAPe fRoM a HiDDeN lOcAtIoN aNd dRiVe PeoPLe cRaZy.

## wHeRe Does It Hurt?

Wrap up some part of your body with bandages. Whenever you're asked what happened, make up a good story. Give everyone a different cause for your "injury" and see how long it takes for people to catch on.

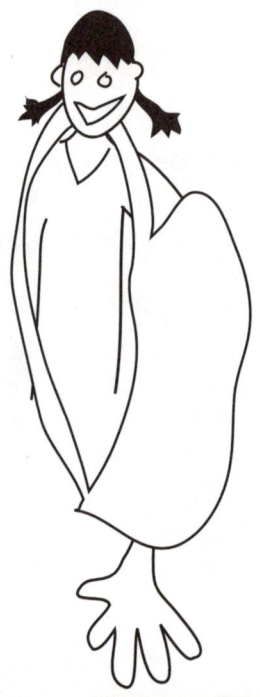

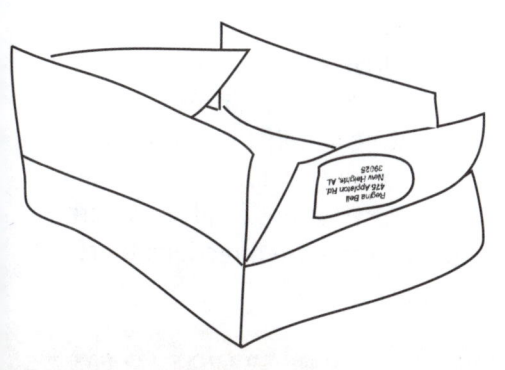

**cReAtE a mYsTerY.** Mail small, unusual objects to all your friends (green marbles, a photo of your favorite hang-out with a cryptic message on the back, three french fries). Be sure to mail one of these mysterious packages to yourself, so you can pretend to be as baffled as everyone else when they're trying to figure out who's responsible for the weirdness.

LoCaTe YoUr hOuSe On a rEaL oLd mAP.

hOw2
dELiA*s

**wHeRe aM I?** Write a series of random directions ("Walk two blocks. Turn left. Pass two mailboxes and turn right." or "Drive approximately five miles on Interstate 95. Get off at next exit. Turn right at next traffic light."). Now choose an equally random starting point, follow your instructions, and see where you end up. Leave the directions there for someone else to find.

PiTcH a tEnT iN tHe LiViNG rOoM. sLeeP tHeRe aNd PLaY a taPe oF nAtuRe sOuNdS.

**LaRGeR ThAn LiFe.** Make a sculpture. Only allow people to view it through a telescope from far away.

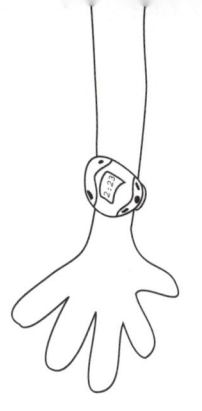

**TiMiNG iS eVeRYtHinG.** Get a group of friends to agree that on a certain day, at exactly the same time, you will all do the same thing—no matter where you happen to be. Sing a Christmas carol in July. Ask the first person you see what they dreamed about last night. Stand on one leg and say the word "kangaroo" ten times. You should plan this one a week in advance so that no one is sure where they'll be at the agreed-upon time.

sEcrEtLY mOw sOmEoNe's LaWn wHeN tHeY'Re nOt hOmE.

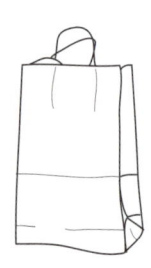

**PaPeR oR PLaStiC?** Carry an empty bag around with you today. Ask various people you know to put something in the bag without showing you what it is. When you get home, study the contents carefully. Try to figure out who gave you each item. Return everything and see if you're right.

PLaNt PLaSTiC tuLiPs aNd rEaL dAiSeS iN YoUr GaRdEn.

**dO I kNoW YoU?** Write a long, personal letter to a total stranger. Tell her what a wonderful person she is, how much she means to you, that the world is a better place with her in it. When it comes to details, be very vague so it's not obvious that you have no idea what you're talking about. Sign with a common name like Bob or Mary and don't put a return address on the envelope.

make a career of it!

# hAiL vIcToRiA!
Remember Blind Man's Bluff and Pin the Tail on the Donkey? They were invented in 19th Century England by the Victorians. One cool Victorian game that's less well-known was called Forfeits. Here are the rules:

One player leaves the room.

Everyone else places a small, personal belonging in a pile.

The first player returns, picks up something from the pile and says "The owner of this thing must..." and then announces something the other player must do unless they want to lose (or "forfeit") their possession. If they refuse, the first player gets to keep it.

Obviously, the amusement level of this game depends on what price people have to pay in order to hold onto their stuff (some suggestions: improvise a song about what you did today or whisper to each player something they don't know about you). The value of the item you offer for ransom is also important—people will do a lot more to keep their watch or their favorite necklace than they will to keep a pack of gum.

hOw2

dELiA*s *

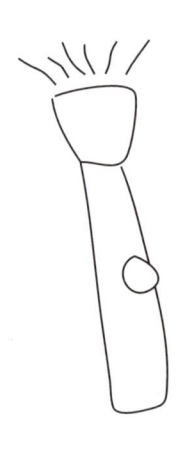

**RoOm FReShEnEr.** Do some fast, easy redecorating. Turn all the pictures in the house upside-down. Move an overstuffed chair from the living room into the kitchen. Cover windows with tin foil. Hang Christmas lights in the bathroom. Replace all your lamps with candles and flashlights.

cOnViNcE YOuR lItTlE sIsTeR tO sEt uP A lEmOnAdE sTaNd iN tHe SnOw.

**BuSY WoRk.** Apply for jobs you don't want, but pretend to take the application process very seriously. Fill out all the forms as strangely as possible. Invent some weird personality quirks for the interview. If, for some unknown reason, you're offered the job, decline politely and say that you've decided to take a job with the CIA instead.

*Here lies Pierre Alberto deep fried friend*

**FeELinG GoTh?** Adopt a gravesite! Go to your local cemetery and find a grave that looks like it's been neglected for a while. Clean the headstone, mow the grass, plant flowers. Think about who the dearly departed might have been, what their life was like, and why their grave has been forsaken. Get spooky and have a chat.

hAvE a biG PiCnIc iN tHe mIdDLe oF YoUr sChOoL GYmNaSiUm.

hOw2

dELiA*s

# hOw₂

**go to dELiAs✷cOm for more
on hOw₂ Waste Time Brilliantly**

**Also by dELiA✷s**
**hOw₂** Write **Love Poems** that Don't Suck
**hOw₂ Understand Your Dreams** and Why Bother

(books available **Back to School 2000**)

**Want to start something?**
Need to know when to stretch the truth?
**Ever thought of hypnotizing your dog?**
Then stay tuned for future books from dELiA✷s.
**Coming Soon!**

If you have any comments or suggestions for other dELiA✷s
hOw₂ books you'd like to see, email us at how2@delias.com